Crittergurumi™

Alex the Axolotl

Alex swims around lake floors and canal bottoms looking for new adventures and friends to hang out with.

SKILL LEVEL
Easy

FINISHED MEASUREMENTS
3 inches wide across Body x 9 inches tall; 5 inches wide across Head with Gills

MATERIALS

- Scheepjes Softfun light (DK) weight cotton/acrylic yarn (1¾ oz/153 yds/50g per ball):
    1 ball each #2513 light rose and #2480 pink or #2530 cloud and #2423 bright turquoise*
    Small amount each #2634 bumblebee, #2480 pink, #2423 bright turquoise and #2412 snow (for Barnacles)
- Size D/3/3.25mm crochet hook or size needed to obtain gauge
- Tapestry needle
- Stitch marker
- 9mm safety eye: 2**
- Black thread
- Polyester fiberfill

*Purchase indicated color pair(s) for the Axolotl(s) of your choice.
**For use by children under 3 years of age, embroider eyes with black thread.

GAUGE
10 sc = 1½ inches; 10 rows = 2 inches

PATTERN NOTES
Instructions given are for first pair of colors; changes for 2nd pair are in brackets.

Pieces are worked separately, then sewn together unless otherwise stated.

All pieces begin with slip ring, chain 1 and indicated number of single crochet worked in ring. Pull gently on beginning tail to close ring after round 1 is completed. If desired, begin instead with 2 chains and indicated number of single crochet worked in 2nd chain from hook.

For pieces worked in continuous rounds, do not join unless instructed to do so. Place marker in first stitch of round and move up as work progresses.

Weave in ends as work progresses.

Leave long yarn tails when fastening off on pieces that will require assembly. Use these tails for sewing.

Stuff firmly, but not so stuffing shows through stitches.

SPECIAL STITCHES
Increase (inc): 2 sc in indicated st.

Invisible single crochet decrease (inv dec): Insert hook in **front lp** *(see Stitch Guide)* of each of next 2 sts, yo, pull up a lp, yo, draw through 2 lps on hook.

AXOLOTL
HEAD & BODY
Rnd 1: Beg at top of Head with light rose [cloud], form a **slip ring** *(see illustration)*, ch 1, 6 sc in ring or **ch 2, 6 sc in 2nd ch from hook** *(see Pattern Notes)*. **Do not join, place marker in first sc** *(see Pattern Notes). (6 sc)*

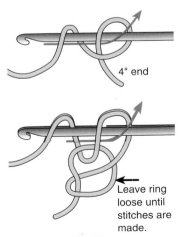

4" end

Leave ring loose until stitches are made.

Slip Ring

Rnd 2: Inc *(see Special Stitches)* in each st around. *(12 sc)*

Rnd 3: [Sc in next sc, inc in next sc] 6 times. *(18 sc)*

Rnd 4: [Sc in next sc, inc in next sc] 9 times. *(27 sc)*

Rnds 5 & 6: Sc in each st around. *(27 sc)*

Rnd 7: Sc in next 2 sc, [sc in next 4 sc, inc in next sc] 6 times. *(32 sc)*

Rnd 8: Rep rnd 5. *(32 sc)*

Rnd 9: Sc in next 2 sc, [sc in next 9 sc, inc in next sc] 3 times. *(35 sc)*

Rnd 10: Rep rnd 5. *(35 sc)*

Rnd 11: Sc in next 15 sc, place first safety eye in last sc made, sc in next 6 sc, place 2nd safety eye in last sc made, sc in next 14 sc. *(35 sc)*

Rnds 12–14: Rep rnd 5. *(35 sc)*

Rnd 15: [Sc in next 5 sc, **inv dec** (see Special Stitches) in next 2 sc] 5 times. *(30 sc)*

Rnds 16 & 17: Rep rnd 5. *(30 sc)*

Rnd 18: [Inv dec in next 2 sc] around. *(15 sc)*

Rnd 19: Sc in next sc, [inv dec in next 2 sc] 7 times. *(8 sc)*

Rnd 20: Inc in each sc around. *(16 sc)*

Rnd 21: Rep rnd 5. *(16 sc)*

Rnd 22: [Sc in next sc, inc in next sc] 8 times. *(24 sc)*

Rnd 23: Rep rnd 5. *(24 sc)*

Rnd 24: [Sc in next 3 sc, inc in next sc] 6 times. *(30 sc)*

Rnds 25 & 26: Rep rnd 5. *(30 sc)*

Rnd 27: [Sc in next 5 sc, inc in next sc] 5 times. *(35 sc)*

Rnds 28–32: Rep rnd 5. *(35 sc)*

Rnd 33: [Sc in next 5 sc, inv dec in next 2 sc] 5 times. *(30 sc)*

Rnds 34–37: Rep rnd 5.

Rnd 38: [Inv dec in next 2 sc] around. *(15 sc)*

Axolotls are only found in one place on Earth. They live in the freshwater Lake Xochimilco and the surrounding waterways near Mexico City, Mexico.
The gills of an axolotl are the feathery-looking protrusions on the sides of its head.

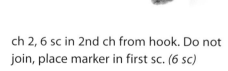

Stuff *(see Pattern Notes)* piece firmly, adding fiberfill as work progresses.

Rnd 39: Rep rnd 5. *(15 sc)*

Rnd 40: [Sc in next 3 sc, inv dec in next 2 sc] 3 times. *(12 sc)*

Rnds 41–46: Rep rnd 5. *(12 sc)*

Rnds 47 & 48: [Inv dec in next 2 sc] around. Fasten off at end of last rnd. *(3 sc)*

GILL
Small Gill
Make 4.

Rnd 1: With pink [bright turquoise], form a slip ring, ch 1, 6 sc in ring or ch 2, 6 sc in 2nd ch from hook. Do not join, place marker in first sc. *(6 sc)*

Rnds 2 & 3: Sc in each sc around. *(6 sc)*

Rnd 4: Inc in each sc around. *(12 sc)*

Rnds 5 & 6: Rep rnd 2. *(12 sc)*

Rnd 7: [Inv dec in next 2 sc] around. **Fasten off** *(see Pattern Notes)*. *(6 sc)*

Large Gill
Make 2.

Rnd 1: With pink [bright turquoise], form a slip ring, ch 1, 6 sc in ring or ch 2, 6 sc in 2nd ch from hook. Do not join, place marker in first sc. *(6 sc)*

Rnds 2 & 3: Sc in each sc around. *(6 sc)*

Rnd 4: Inc in each sc around. *(12 sc)*

Rnd 5: [Sc in next sc, inc in next sc] 6 times. *(18 sc)*

Rnds 6 & 7: Rep rnd 2. *(18 sc)*

Rnd 8: [Inv dec in next 2 sc] around. *(9 sc)*

Rnd 9: Rep rnd 2. Fasten off. *(9 sc)*

FIN
Dorsal Fin

Row 1: Ch 50, sc in 2nd ch from hook and in each ch across, turn. *(49 sc)*

Row 2: Ch 3, sc in first sc, [sk next sc, ch 4, sc in next sc] 23 times, sc in last sc. Fasten off. *(25 sc, 23 ch-4 sps)*

Tail Fin

Row 1: With pink [bright turquoise], ch 20, sc in 2nd ch from hook and in each ch across, turn. *(19 sc)*

Row 2: Ch 6, sc in first sc, [sk next sc, ch 6, sc in next sc] 9 times. Fasten off. *(10 sc, 10 ch-6 sps)*

LEG
Make 4.

Rnd 1: Beg at bottom of Leg with light rose [cloud], form a slip ring, ch 1, 6 sc in ring or ch 2, 6 sc in 2nd ch from hook. Do not join, place marker in first sc. *(6 sc)*

Rnd 2: [Sc in next sc, inc in next sc, sc in next sc] twice. *(8 sc)*

Rnds 3–7: Sc in each sc around. Fasten off. *(8 sc)*

BARNACLE
Small Patch

Make 1 each with snow and bumblebee [bright turquoise and pink].

Form a slip ring, ch 1, 6 sc in ring or ch 2, 6 sc in 2nd ch from hook. Fasten off. *(6 sc)*

Large Patch

Rnd 1: With pink [bumblebee], form a slip ring, ch 1, 6 sc in ring or ch 2, 6 sc in 2nd ch from hook. Do not join, place marker in first sc. *(6 sc)*

Rnd 2: [Sc in next sc, inc in next sc] 3 times. Fasten off. *(9 sc)*

ASSEMBLY & FINISHING

Refer to photo as a guide for placement of pieces.

Positioning one end at top of Head and other end slightly above bottom of tail, center Dorsal Fin on back and pin in place. With end tail, sew across Head and Body.

Position and pin Tail Fin evenly around tail, sew in place.

Stuff Legs, then pin to sides of Body and sew in place.

With black thread, embroider small **backstitches** *(see illustration)* for mouth and eyebrows.

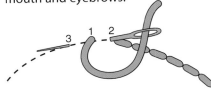

Backstitch

Position each Large Gill between 2 Small Gills on sides of Head, sew in place. ●

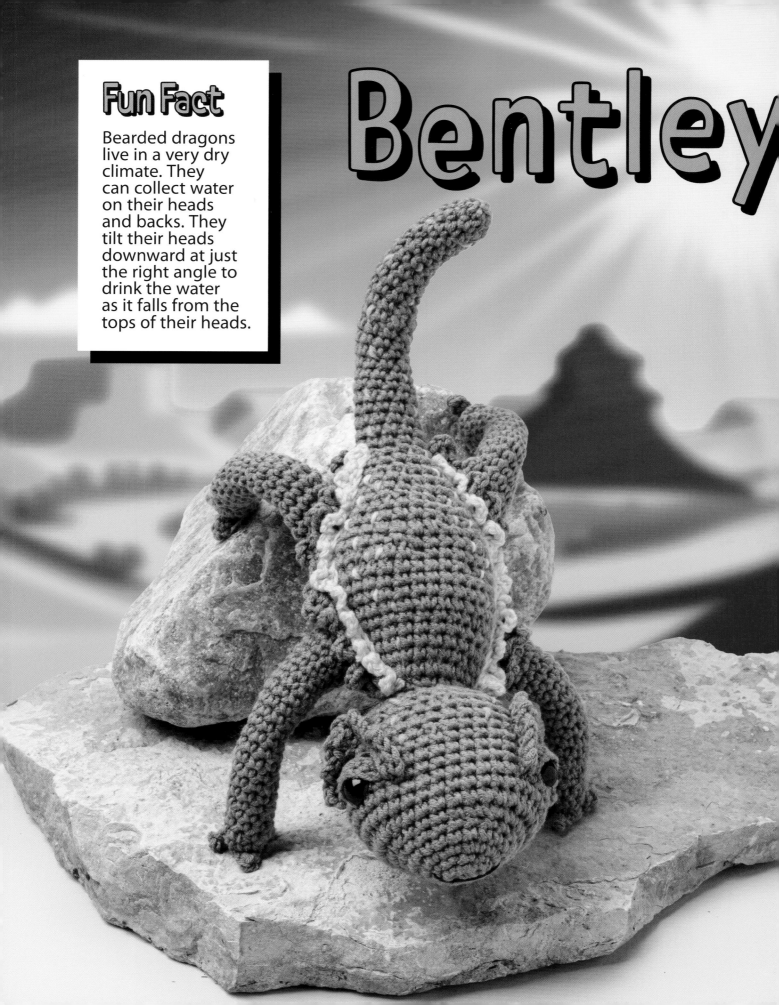

Bentley

the Bearded Dragon

Bentley spends his day basking in the sun, soaking up the heat and climbing rocks around the desert.

SKILL LEVEL
Easy

FINISHED MEASUREMENTS
3½ inches wide across Body x 11 inches long

MATERIALS

3 LIGHT

- Scheepjes Softfun light (DK) weight cotton/acrylic yarn (1¾ oz/153 yds/50g per ball):
    1 ball each #2531 olive and #2634 bumblebee
    Small amount #2621 mustard (for stitching)
- Size D/3/3.25mm crochet hook or size needed to obtain gauge
- Tapestry needle
- Stitch marker
- 12mm black safety eye: 2*
- 11-inch-long 9-gauge wire: 2 pieces
- Black thread
- Sewing pins
- Polyester fiberfill

For use by children under 3 years of age, embroider eyes with black thread.

GAUGE
10 sc = 1½ inches; 10 rows = 2 inches

PATTERN NOTES
Pieces are worked separately then sewn together unless otherwise stated.

For pieces beginning with a slip ring, chain 1 and work indicated number of single crochet in ring. Pull gently on beginning tail to close ring after round 1 is completed. If desired, begin instead with 2 chains and indicated number of single crochet worked in 2nd chain from hook.

For pieces worked in continuous rounds, do not join unless instructed to do so. Place marker in first stitch of round and move up as work progresses.

Stuff firmly, but not so the stuffing shows through the stitches.

Leave long tails when fastening off on pieces that will require assembly. Use these tails for sewing.

SPECIAL STITCHES
Increase (inc): 2 sc in indicated st.

Invisible single crochet decrease (inv dec): Insert hook in **front lp** *(see Stitch Guide)* of next 2 sts, yo, pull up a lp, yo, draw through 2 lps on hook.

BEARDED DRAGON

HEAD & BODY
Rnd 1: Beg at tip of nose with olive, form a **slip ring** *(see illustration)*, 6 sc in ring or **ch 2, 6 sc in 2nd ch from hook** *(see Pattern Notes)*. **Do not join, place marker in first sc** *(see Pattern Notes). (6 sc)*

4" end

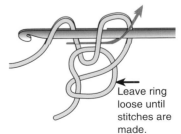
Leave ring loose until stitches are made.

Slip Ring

Rnd 2: [Inc (*see Special Stitches*) in next sc, sc in next sc] 3 times. (*9 sc*)

Rnd 3: Inc in each sc around. (*18 sc*)

Rnds 4 & 5: Sc in each sc around. (*18 sc*)

Rnd 6: Inc in next 5 sc, sc in next 5 sc, inc in next 5 sc, sc in next 3 sc. (*28 sc*)

Rnd 7: Sc in next 3 sc, inc in next 4 sc, sc in next 9 sc, inc in next 4 sc, sc in next 8 sc. (*36 sc*)

Rnds 8 & 9: Rep rnd 4. (*36 sc*)

Rnd 10: Sc in next 9 sc, place first safety eye in last sc made, sc in next 14 sc, place 2nd safety eye in last sc made, sc in next 13 sc. (*36 sc*)

Rnds 11 & 12: Rep rnd 4. (*36 sc*)

Rnd 13: [Sc in next 4 sc, **inv dec** (*see Special Stitches*) in next 2 sc] 6 times. (*30 sc*)

Rnds 14 & 15: Rep rnd 4. (*30 sc*)

Rnd 16: [Sc in next 3 sc, inv dec in next 2 sc] 6 times. (*24 sc*)

Rnd 17: Rep rnd 4. (*24 sc*)

Rnd 18: [Inv dec in next 2 sc] around. (*12 sc*)

Rnd 19: [Inc in next sc, sc in next sc] 6 times. (*18 sc*)

Rnd 20: [Sc in next 2 sc, inc in next sc] 6 times. (*24 sc*)

Rnds 21 & 22: Rep rnd 4. (*24 sc*)

Rnd 23: [Sc in next 5 sc, inc in next sc] 4 times. (*28 sc*)

Rnd 24: Rep rnd 4. (*28 sc*)

Rnd 25: Sc in next 4 sc, [sc in next 5 sc, inc in next sc] 4 times. (*32 sc*)

Rnds 26 & 27: Rep rnd 4. (*32 sc*)

Rnd 28: Sc in next 2 sc, [sc in next 9 sc, inc in next sc] 3 times. (*35 sc*)

Rnd 29: Rep rnd 4. (*35 sc*)

Stuff (*see Pattern Notes*) piece firmly, adding fiberfill as work progresses as needed.

Rnd 30: [Sc in next 5 sc, inv dec in next 2 sc] 5 times. (*30 sc*)

Rnds 31–33: Rep rnd 4. (*30 sc*)

Rnd 34: [Sc in next 3 sc, inv dec in next 2 sc] 6 times. (*24 sc*)

Rnds 35 & 36: Rep rnd 4. (*24 sc*)

Rnd 37: [Sc in next 2 sc, inv dec in next 2 sc] 6 times. (*18 sc*)

Rnd 38: [Sc in next sc, inv dec in next 2 sc] 6 times. (*12 sc*)

Rnds 39–45: Rep rnd 4. (*12 sc*)

Rnd 46: Sc in next 4 sc, inv dec in next 2 sc, sc in next 6 sc. (*11 sc*)

Rnds 47–55: Rep rnd 4. (*11 sc*)

Rnd 56: Inv dec in next 2 sc, sc in next 9 sc. (*10 sc*)

Rnds 57–60: Rep rnd 4. (*10 sc*)

Rnd 61: [Inv dec in next 2 sc] around. (*5 sc*)

Rnd 62: [Inv dec in next 2 sc] twice, sk last st. Fasten off. (*2 sc*)

LEG
Make 4.

Rnd 1: Beg at bottom of Leg with olive, form a slip ring, 6 sc in ring or ch 2, 6 sc in 2nd ch from hook. (*6 sc*)

Rnd 2: [Inc in next sc, sc in next 2 sc] twice. (*8 sc*)

Rnds 3–11: Sc in each sc around. (*8 sc*)

Rnd 12: [Sc in next 3 sc, inc in next sc] twice. (*10 sc*)

Rnds 13–16: Rep rnd 3. (*10 sc*)

Rnd 17: [Sc in next 4 sc, inc in next sc] twice. (*12 sc*)

Rnds 18–20: Rep rnd 3. (*12 sc*)

Fasten off (*see Pattern Notes*).

EYELID
Make 2.

With olive, ch 6, sc in 2nd ch from hook and each ch across. Fasten off. (*5 sc*)

BODY TRIM
Make 2 in olive and 2 in bumblebee.

Ch 22, (sc, ch 4, sc) in 2nd ch from hook, [sk next ch, (sc, ch 4, sc) in next ch] 10 times. Fasten off. (*11 ch-4 lps*)

EYE TRIM
Make 2.

With olive, ch 16, (sc, ch 2, sc) in 2nd ch from hook, [sk next ch, (sc, ch 2, sc) in next ch] 7 times. Fasten off. (*8 ch-2 lps*)

FOOT
Make 4.

With olive, ch 4, sl st in 2nd ch from hook, [ch 3, sl st in 2nd and 3rd chs from hook] 3 times, sl st in first ch to join. Fasten off. (*4 toes*)

ASSEMBLY & FINISHING

Stuff Legs.

Refer to photo as a guide for placement of pieces.

Position and pin Eyelids up against eyes and Eye Trim in a sideways V-shape behind Eyelids. With end tail, sew in place.

Put wires through Body, 1 for front Legs and 1 for back Legs, bend each end so there are no sharp points, slide Legs over wire and sew in place.

Position and pin Body Trim across each side of Body, just above Legs, with olive Trims below bumblebee Trims, sew in place.

With bumblebee and mustard, embroider small **backstitches** (see illustration) onto Body to create small spots. With black thread, embroider small eyebrows in space between Eyelid and Eye Trim.

Backstitch

Sew 1 Foot on end of each Leg.

Weave in rem ends. ●

Greta the Guinea Pig

SKILL LEVEL
Easy

FINISHED MEASUREMENTS
3½ inches wide across Body x 5 inches long

MATERIALS
- Scheepjes Softfun light (DK) weight cotton/acrylic yarn (1¾ oz/153 yds/50g per ball): 1 ball each #2621 mustard and #2412 snow, #2533 wheat and #2491 pecan or #2530 cloud and #2491 pecan*

- Size D/3/3.25mm crochet hook or size needed to obtain gauge
- Tapestry needle
- Stitch markers: 2
- 12mm safety eye: 2**
- Black thread
- Sewing pins
- Polyester fiberfill

*Purchase indicated color pair(s) for the Guinea Pig(s) of your choice.
**For use by children under 3 years of age, embroider eyes with black thread.

GAUGE
10 sc = 1½ inches; 10 rows = 2 inches

PATTERN NOTES
Instructions given are for first Guinea Pig; changes for 2nd and 3rd Guinea Pigs are in brackets.

Pieces are worked separately then sewn together unless otherwise stated.

All pieces begin with slip ring, chain 1 and indicated number of single crochet worked in ring. Pull gently on beginning tail to close ring after round 1 is completed. If desired, begin instead with 2 chains and indicated number of single crochet worked in 2nd chain from hook.

All pieces are worked in continuous rounds; do not join unless instructed to do so. Place marker in first stitch of round and move up as work progresses.

To change color in indicated single crochet, work last yarn over with **new color** *(see illustration)*. Drop color not in use to back of work and loosely carry over when next needed. Do not fasten off until instructed. Tie off

Greta and her siblings love to eat and would spend all day munching away in your garden if they could!

snow [pecan, pecan] on inside after fastening off.

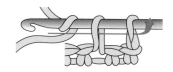

Single Crochet Color Change

Leave long tails when fastening off on pieces which will require assembly. Use these tails for sewing.

Stuff firmly, but not so the stuffing shows through the stitches.

SPECIAL STITCHES
Increase (inc): 2 sc in indicated st.

Invisible single crochet decrease (inv dec): Insert hook in front lp of next 2 sts, yo, pull up a lp, yo, draw through 2 lps on hook.

GUINEA PIG

HEAD & BODY

Rnd 1: Beg at tip of nose with mustard [wheat, cloud], form a **slip ring** (see illustration), 6 sc in ring or **ch 2, 6 sc in 2nd ch from hook** (see Pattern Notes). **Do not join, place marker in first sc** (see Pattern Notes). (6 sc)

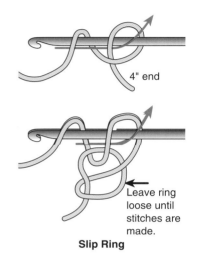

Slip Ring

4" end

Leave ring loose until stitches are made.

Rnd 2: [**Inc** (see Special Stitches) in next sc, sc in next 2 sc] twice. (8 sc)

Rnd 3: Inc in each sc around. (16 sc)

Rnd 4: Inc in next 4 sc, sc in next 12 sc, **sc color change** (see Pattern Notes) to snow [pecan, pecan] in last st. (20 sc)

Rnd 5: Inc in next 3 sc, change to mustard [wheat, cloud] in last st, sc in next 6 sc, change to snow [pecan, pecan] in last st, sc in next 6 sc, change to mustard [wheat, cloud] in last st, sc in next 5 sc, change to snow [pecan, pecan] in last st. (23 sc)

Rnd 6: Sc in next 5 sc, change to mustard [wheat, cloud] in last st, sc in next 3 sc, inc in next 4 sc, sc in next sc, change to snow [pecan, pecan] in last st, sc in next 5 sc, change to mustard [wheat, cloud] in last st, sc in next 5 sc, change to snow [pecan, pecan] in last st. (27 sc)

Rnd 7: Sc in next 4 sc, place first safety eye in last sc made, sc in next sc, change to mustard [wheat, cloud] in last st, sc in next 12 sc, change to snow [pecan, pecan] in last st, sc in next 4 sc, place 2nd safety eye in last sc made, sc in next sc, change to mustard [wheat, cloud] in last st, sc in next 5 sc. (27 sc)

Rnd 8: Sc in next sc, change to snow [pecan, pecan] in last st, sc in next 3 sc, change to mustard [wheat, cloud] in last st, sc in next 14 sc, change to snow [pecan, pecan] in last st, sc in next 3 sc, change mustard [wheat, cloud] in last st, sc in next 6 sc. (27 sc)

Rnds 9–11: With mustard [wheat, cloud] throughout, sc in each sc around. (27 sc)

Rnd 12: Inc in next 2 sc, sc in next 10 sc, inc in next sc, sc in next 11 sc, place new stitch marker in last sc (top of head), inc in next sc, sc in next sc, inc in next sc. (32 sc)

Rnd 13: Sc in next 24 sc, change to snow [pecan, pecan] in last st, sc in next 5 sc, change to mustard [wheat, cloud] in last st, sc in next 3 sc. (32 sc)

Rnd 14: Sc in next 25 sc, change to snow [pecan, pecan] in last st, sc in next 4 sc, change to mustard [wheat, cloud] in last st, sc in next 3 sc. (32 sc)

Rnd 15: [Sc in next 5 sc, inc in next sc] 4 times, sc in next 2 sc, change to snow [pecan, pecan] in last st, sc in next 3 sc, change to mustard [wheat, cloud] in last st, sc in next 3 sc. (36 sc)

Fun Facts

Guinea pigs do not sweat. They have teeth that are constantly growing, which means they need to munch on food a lot to help wear them down. Guinea pigs eat their own poop!

Rnd 16: Rep rnd 9. *(36 sc)*

Rnd 17: [Sc in next 5 sc, inc in next sc] 6 times. *(42 sc)*

Rnd 18: Sc in next 6 sc, change to snow [pecan, pecan] in last st, sc in next 6 sc, change to mustard [wheat, cloud] in last st, sc in next 30 sc. *(42 sc)*

Rnd 19: Sc in next 8 sc, change to snow [pecan, pecan] in last st, sc in next 4 sc, change to mustard [wheat, cloud] in last st, sc in next 30 sc. *(42 sc)*

Rnd 20: Sc in next 7 sc, change to snow [pecan, pecan] in last st, sc in next 8 sc, change to mustard [wheat, cloud] in last st, sc in next 27 sc. *(42 sc)*

Rnds 21 & 22: Sc in next 6 sc, change to snow [pecan, pecan] in last st, sc in next 12 sc, change to mustard [wheat, cloud] in last st, sc in next 24 sc. *(42 sc)*

Rnd 23: Inc in next 2 sc, sc in next 4 sc, change to snow [pecan, pecan] in last st, sc in next 19 sc, change to mustard [wheat, cloud] in last st, sc in next 17 sc. *(44 sc)*

Rnd 24: Sc in next 7 sc, change to snow [pecan, pecan] in last st, sc in next 20 sc, change to mustard [wheat, cloud] in last st, sc in next 17 sc. *(44 sc)*

Rnd 25: Sc in next 10 sc, change to snow [pecan, pecan] in last st, sc in next 14 sc, change to mustard [wheat,

cloud] in last st, sc in next 20 sc. *(44 sc)*

Rnd 26: Sc in next 13 sc, change to snow [pecan, pecan] in last st, sc in next 10 sc, change to mustard [wheat, cloud] in last st, sc in next 21 sc. **Fasten off** *(see Pattern Notes)* snow [pecan, pecan]. *(44 sc)*

Rnds 27 & 28: Rep rnd 9. *(44 sc)*

Rnd 29: [Inv dec in next 2 sc] around. *(22 sc)*

Rnd 30: Rep rnd 9. *(22 sc)*

Rnd 31: Rep rnd 29. *(11 sc)*

Rnd 32: Rep rnd 9. *(11 sc)*

Rnd 33: [Inv dec in next 2 sc] 5 times, sc in next sc. *(6 sc)*

Stuff *(see Pattern Notes)* piece firmly.

Rnd 34: Rep rnd 29. *(3 sc)*

Rnd 35: Inv dec in next 2 sts, sk last st. Fasten off. *(2 sc)*

EAR
Make 2.

Rnd 1: Beg at tip of Ear with snow [pecan, pecan], form a slip ring, 6 sc in ring or ch 2, 6 sc in 2nd ch from hook. *(6 sc)*

Rnd 2: [Inc in next sc, sc in next sc] 3 times. *(9 sc)*

Rnds 3–5: Sc in next 9 sc. *(9 sc)*

Fasten off.

LEG
Make 4.

Rnd 1: Beg at bottom of Leg with mustard [wheat, cloud], form a slip ring, 6 sc in ring or ch 2, 6 sc in 2nd ch from hook. *(6 sc)*

Rnd 2: [Inc in next sc, sc in next 2 sc] twice. *(8 sc)*

Rnds 3–7: Sc in each sc around. *(8 sc)*

Fasten off.

ASSEMBLY & FINISHING

Do not stuff Legs or Ears.

Refer to photo as a guide for placement of pieces.

Position and pin each Ear about 4 rows behind eye. With end tail, sew in place. Position and pin 4 legs on underside of Body, sew in place.

With black thread, embroider **straight stitches** *(see illustration)* for eyebrows, nose and mouth.

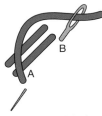

Straight Stitch

Weave in rem ends. ●

Homer the

Fun Fact

Despite their name, hermit crabs are very social and live in large groups.

Hermit Crab

Homer and his siblings are excited to be in their new homes and look forward to getting into all kinds of family shenanigans.

SKILL LEVEL
Easy

FINISHED MEASUREMENTS
3½ inches wide across Body x 7 inches tall

MATERIALS
- Scheepjes Softfun light (DK) weight cotton/acrylic yarn (1¾ oz/153 yds/50g per ball):
  1 ball each #2410 candy apple and #2639 green tea, #2410 candy apple and #2621 mustard or #2652 cantaloupe and #2625 sea mist*
  Small amount each #2634 bumblebee, #2621 mustard, #2625 sea mist, #2535 forest and #2652 cantaloupe (for Barnacles)
- Size D/3/3.25mm crochet hook or size needed to obtain gauge
- Tapestry needle
- Stitch marker
- 9mm safety eye: 2**
- Black thread
- Polyester fiberfill
- 11-inch-long pieces of 9-gauge wire: 2

*Purchase indicated color pair(s) for the Crab(s) of your choice.
**For use by children under 3 years of age, embroider eyes with black thread.*

GAUGE
10 sc = 1½ inches; 10 rows = 2 inches

PATTERN NOTES
Instructions given are for first hermit crab; changes for 2nd and 3rd hermit crabs are in brackets. Where only 1 color is given, it applies to all hermit crabs.

Pieces are worked separately, then sewn together unless otherwise stated.

All pieces begin with slip ring, chain 1 and indicated number of single crochet worked in ring. Pull gently on beginning tail to close ring after round 1 is completed. If desired, begin instead with 2 chains and indicated number of single crochet worked in 2nd chain from hook.

Work in continuous rounds; do not join unless instructed to do so. Place marker in first stitch of round and move up as work progresses.

Weave in ends as work progresses.

Leave long tails for sewing when fastening off pieces which require assembly.

Stuff firmly, but not so stuffing shows through stitches.

SPECIAL STITCHES
Increase (inc): 2 sc in indicated st.

Invisible single crochet decrease (inv dec): Insert hook in **front lp** (see Stitch Guide) of next 2 sts, yo, pull up a lp, yo, draw through 2 lps on hook.

HERMIT CRAB

EYE
Make 2.

Rnd 1: Beg at top of Eye with candy apple [candy apple, cantaloupe], form a **slip ring** (see illustration), ch 1, 6 sc in ring or **ch 2, 6 sc in 2nd ch from hook** (see Pattern Notes). **Do not join, place marker in first sc** (see Pattern Notes). (6 sc)

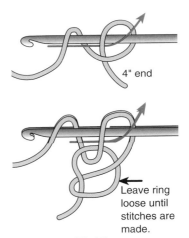

Slip Ring

Rnd 2: Inc (see Special Stitches) in each st around. (12 sc)

Rnd 3: Sc in each st around. (12 sc)

Rnd 4: [Sc in next sc, inc in next sc] 6 times. (18 sc)

Rnds 5 & 6: Rep rnd 3. (18 sc)

Rnd 7: Sc in next 8 sc, place safety eye in last sc made, sc in next 10 sc. (18 sc)

Rnds 8–12: Rep rnd 3. (18 sc)

Rnd 13: Sc in next 2 sc, [sc in next 3 sc, inc in next sc] 4 times. **Fasten off** (see Pattern Notes). *(22 sc)*

BODY

Rnd 1: Beg at top of Body with candy apple [candy apple, cantaloupe], form a slip ring, ch 1, 6 sc in ring or ch 2, 6 sc in 2nd ch from hook. Do not join, place marker in first sc. *(6 sc)*

Rnd 2: Inc in each sc around. *(12 sc)*

Rnd 3: [Sc in next sc, inc in next sc] 6 times. *(18 sc)*

Rnd 4: [Sc in next sc, inc in next sc] 9 times. *(27 sc)*

Rnd 5: Sc in next sc, [sc in next sc, inc in next sc] 13 times. *(40 sc)*

Rnd 6: Sc in each st around. *(40 sc)*

Rnd 7: [Sc in next 7 sc, inc in next sc] 5 times. *(45 sc)*

Rnds 8–11: Rep rnd 6. *(45 sc)*

Rnd 12: [Sc in next 3 sc, **inv dec** (see Special Stitches) in next 2 sc] 9 times. *(36 sc)*

Rnds 13 & 14: Rep rnd 6. *(36 sc)*

Rnd 15: [Inv dec in next 2 sc] around. *(18 sc)*

Stuff (see Pattern Notes) firmly.

Rnd 16: [Inv dec in next 2 sc] around. *(9 sc)*

Rnd 17: [Inv dec in next 2 sc] twice, sc in next sc. *(5 sc)*

Rnd 18: Sc in next sc, [inv dec in next 2 sc] twice. Leaving 6-inch tail, fasten off. *(3 sc)*

FRONT LEG
Make 2.

Rnd 1: Beg at top of Front Leg with candy apple [candy apple, cantaloupe], form a slip ring, 6 sc in ring or ch 2, 6 sc in 2nd ch from hook. Do not join, place marker in first sc. *(6 sc)*

Rnds 2 & 3: Sc in each sc around. *(6 sc)*

Rnd 4: Inc in next 3 sc, sc in next 3 sc. *(9 sc)*

Rnd 5: Inc in next 6 sc, sc in next 3 sc. *(15 sc)*

Rnds 6 & 7: Rep rnd 2. *(15 sc)*

Rnd 8: Sc in next 11 sc, [inv dec in next 2 sc] twice. *(13 sc)*

Rnd 9: Sc in next 9 sc, [inv dec in next 2 sc] twice. *(11 sc)*

Rnds 10–15: Rep rnd 2. *(11 sc)*

Rnd 16: Sc in next 2 sc, [sc in next sc, inv dec in next 2 sc] 3 times. Fasten off. *(8 sc)*

Pincer
Make 2.

Rnd 1: Beg at tip of Pincer with candy apple [candy apple, cantaloupe], form a slip ring, 6 sc in ring or ch 2, 6 sc in 2nd ch from hook. Do not join, place marker in first sc. *(6 sc)*

Rnd 2: Sc in each sc around. *(6 sc)*

Rnd 3: [Sc in next sc, inc in next sc] 3 times. *(9 sc)*

Rnd 4: Rep rnd 2. Fasten off. *(9 sc)*

BACK LEG
Make 2.

Rnd 1: Beg at tip of Back Leg with candy apple [candy apple, cantaloupe], form a slip ring, 6 sc in ring or ch 2, 6 sc in 2nd ch from hook. Do not join, place marker in first sc. *(6 sc)*

Rnd 2: [Sc in next sc, inc in next sc] 3 times. *(9 sc)*

Rnds 3–11: Sc in each sc around. Fasten off. *(9 sc)*

SHELL

Rnd 1: Beg at top of Shell with green tea [mustard, sea mist], form a slip

ring, 6 sc in ring or ch 2, 6 sc in 2nd ch from hook. Do not join, place marker in first sc. *(6 sc)*

Rnds 2 & 3: Sc in each sc around. *(6 sc)*

Rnd 4: Inc in each sc around. *(12 sc)*

Rnd 5: Rep rnd 2. *(12 sc)*

Rnd 6: [Sc in next sc, inc in next sc] 6 times. *(18 sc)*

Rnd 7: Rep rnd 2. *(18 sc)*

Rnd 8: [Sc in next sc, inc in next sc] 9 times. *(27 sc)*

Rnd 9: Rep rnd 2. *(27 sc)*

Rnd 10: Sc in next sc, [inv dec in next sc] 13 times. *(14 sc)*

Rnd 11: Rep rnd 2. *(14 sc)*

Rnd 12: Inc in each sc around. *(28 sc)*

Rnd 13: [Sc in next sc, inc in next sc] 14 times. *(42 sc)*

Rnds 14–19: Rep rnd 2. *(42 sc)*

Rnd 20: [Inv dec in next 2 sc] around. *(21 sc)*

Rnd 21: Rep rnd 2. *(42 sc)*

Rnd 22: Sc in next 2 sc, [sc in next 3 sc, inc in next sc] 10 times. *(52 sc)*

Rnds 23–25: Rep rnd 2. *(52 sc)*

Rnd 26: Inv dec in next 2 sc, [sc in next 3 sc, inv dec in next 2 sc] 10 times. *(41 sc)*

Rnd 27: Sc in next sc, [inv dec in next 2 sc] 20 times. Fasten off. *(21 sc)*

BARNACLE
Small Patch

With sea mist [jade, olive], form a slip ring, 6 sc in ring or ch 2, 6 sc in 2nd ch from hook. Fasten off. *(6 sc)*

Large Patch

Rnd 1: With cantaloupe [bumblebee, mustard], form a slip ring, 6 sc in ring

or ch 2, 6 sc in 2nd ch from hook. Do not join, place marker in first sc. *(6 sc)*

Rnd 2: [Sc in next sc, inc in next sc] 3 times. Fasten off. *(9 sc)*

ASSEMBLY & FINISHING

Stuff all pieces.

Refer to photo as a guide for placement of pieces.

Insert wire in Body where Front Legs will be placed. Bend ends of each wire so there are no sharp points. Place Front Legs over wires and sew in place. Sew Pincers to top of Front Legs.

Sew Barnacles to Shell.

Sew Eyes to top of Body. Angle Shell on back of Body and sew in place.

Sew Back Legs toward back of Body under Shell.

With black thread, embroider small **straight stitches** *(see illustration)* for mouth and eyebrows. ●

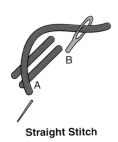

Straight Stitch

Fun Facts

Budgie is short for budgerigar. Budgies have monocular vision. They can move and see out of each eye independently of the other.

Beauregard the Budgie

SKILL LEVEL
Easy

FINISHED MEASUREMENTS
3½ inches wide at bottom of Body x 5 inches tall

MATERIALS
- Scheepjes Softfun light (DK) weight cotton/acrylic yarn (1¾ oz/153 yds/50g per ball):
  1 ball each #2634 bumblee, #2423 bright turquiose and #2530 cloud; #2530 cloud, #2535 forest and #2621 mustard; or #2423 bright turquiose and #2513 light rose
  Small amount #2652 cantaloupe*
- Size D/3/3.25mm crochet hook or size needed to obtain gauge
- Tapestry needle
- Stitch marker
- 8mm safety eye: 2**
- Sewing pins
- Black thread
- Polyester fiberfill

*Purchase indicated color group(s) for the Budgie(s) of your choice.
**For use by children under 3 years of age, embroider eyes with black thread.

GAUGE
10 sc = 1½ inches; 10 rows = 2 inches

PATTERN NOTES
Instructions given are for first Budgie; changes for 2nd and 3rd Budgies are in brackets. Where only 1 color is given, it applies to all Budgies.

Pieces are worked separately then sewn together unless otherwise stated.

All pieces except Beak and Foot begin with slip ring, chain 1 and indicated number of single crochet worked in ring. Pull gently on beginning tail to close ring after round 1 is completed. If desired, begin instead with 2 chains and indicated number of single crochet worked in 2nd chain from hook.

All pieces except Beak and Foot are worked in continuous rounds; do not join unless instructed to do so. Place marker in first stitch of round and move up as work progresses.

To change color in indicated single crochet, work last yarn over with **new color** (see illustration). Drop color not in use to back of work until next needed.

Beauregard and his friends get a kick out of mimicking their human owners, so be wary of what you say in their presence.

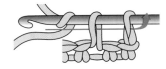

Single Crochet Color Change

Join with slip stitch as indicated unless otherwise stated.

Stuff firmly, but not so the stuffing shows through the stitches.

Leave long tails when fastening off on pieces that will require assembly. Use these tails for sewing.

SPECIAL STITCHES
Increase (inc): 2 sc in indicated st.

Invisible single crochet decrease (inv dec): Insert hook in front lp of next 2 sts, yo, pull up a lp, yo, draw through 2 lps on hook.

BUDGIE

HEAD & BODY

Rnd 1: Beg at top of head with **bumblebee [light turquoise, cloud]** (see Pattern Notes), form a **slip ring** (see illustration), 6 sc in ring or **ch 2, 6 sc in 2nd ch from hook** (see Pattern Notes). **Do not join, place marker in first sc** (see Pattern Notes). (6 sc)

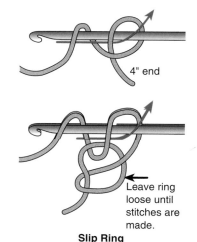

4" end

Leave ring loose until stitches are made.

Slip Ring

Rnd 2: Inc (see Special Stitches) in each sc around. (12 sc)

Rnd 3: [Sc in next sc, inc in next sc] 6 times. (18 sc)

Rnd 4: Sc in each sc around. (18 sc)

Rnd 5: [Sc in next sc, inc in next sc] 9 times. (27 sc)

Rnds 6–8: Rep rnd 4. (27 sc)

Rnd 9: [Sc in next 8 sc, inc in next sc] 3 times. (30 sc)

Rnd 10: Sc in next 13 sc, place first safety eye in last sc made, sc in next 8 sc, place 2nd safety eye in last sc made, sc in next 9 sc. (30 sc)

Rnd 11: [Sc in next 8 sc, **inv dec** (see Special Stitches) in next 2 sc] 3 times. (27 sc)

Rnd 12: Sc in next 15 sc, inv dec in next 2 sc, sc in next 10 sc. (26 sc)

Rnd 13: Rep rnd 4, **sc color change** (see Pattern Notes) to bright turquoise [light rose, forest] in last st. Fasten off bumblebee [light turquoise, cloud]. (26 sc)

Rnds 14 & 15: Rep rnd 4. (26 sc)

Rnd 16: Sc in next sc, inc in next 4 sc, sc in next 8 sc, inv dec in next 2 sc, sc in next 4 sc, inv dec in next 2 sc, sc in next 5 sc. (28 sc)

Rnds 17 & 18: Rep rnd 4. (28 sc)

Rnd 19: Sc in next 4 sc, inc in next 3 sc, sc in next 21 sc. (31 sc)

Rnd 20: Rep rnd 4. (31 sc)

Rnd 21: Sc in next 6 sc, inc in next 2 sc, sc in next 23 sc. (33 sc)

Rnds 22 & 23: Rep rnd 4. (33 sc)

Rnd 24: Sc in next 7 sc, inc in next sc, sc in next 2 sc, inc in next sc, sc in next 12 sc, inc in next sc, sc in next 6 sc, inc in next sc, sc in next 2 sc. (37 sc)

Rnd 25: Rep rnd 4. (37 sc)

Rnd 26: Sc in next 2 sc, [sc in next 6 sc, inc in next sc] 5 times. (42 sc)

Rnds 27–29: Rep rnd 4. (42 sc)

Rnd 30: Sc in next sc, [inv dec in next 2 sc] 4 times, sc in next 10 sc, [inv dec in next 2 sc] 11 times, sc in next sc. (27 sc)

Rnd 31: Rep rnd 4. (27 sc)

Rnd 32: [Inv dec in next 2 sc] 4 times, sc in next 4 sc, [inv dec in next 2 sc] 7 times, sc in next sc. (16 sc)

Stuff (see Pattern Notes) piece firmly.

Rnds 33–35: [Inv dec in next 2 sc] around. (2 sc)

Fasten off.

WING

Make 2.

Rnd 1: Beg in middle of wing with bumblebee [light rose, mustard], form a slip ring, 6 sc in ring or ch 2, 6 sc in 2nd ch from hook. (6 sc)

Rnd 2: Inc in each sc around. (12 sc)

Rnd 3: [Sc in next sc, inc in next sc] 6 times. (18 sc)

Rnd 4: [Sc in next 2 sc, inc in next sc] 6 times. (24 sc)

Rnd 5: [Sc in next sc, inc in next sc] 12 times. (36 sc)

Row 6: Fold Wing in half with working lp on right-hand edge, working through both sides at the same time, sc in next 18 sc to join sides and create a half circle. Fasten off. (18 sc)

Trim

Row 7: Leaving a long beg tail on first Wing only, **join** (see Pattern Notes) cloud [light turquoise, forest] in first sc, (sc, ch 3, sc) in same sc as join, [sk next sc, (sc, ch 3, sc) in next sc] 8 times, sk last sc. **Fasten off** (see Pattern Notes), leaving a long tail on 2nd Wing only. (18 sc, 9 ch-3 lps)

TAIL

Rnd 1: Beg at tip of tail with bumblebee [light rose, cloud], form a slip ring, 6 sc in ring or ch 2, 6 sc in 2nd ch from hook. (6 sc)

Rnd 2: Inc in each sc around. (12 sc)

Rnds 3–7: Sc in each sc around. (12 sc)

Rnd 8: [Sc in next sc, inc in next sc] 6 times. (18 sc)

Rnds 9–12: Rep rnd 3. *(18 sc)*

Rnd 13: [Sc in next 5 sc, inc in next sc] 3 times. *(21 sc)*

Rnds 14–17: Rep rnd 3. *(21 sc)*

Rnd 18: Rep rnd 3, sc color change to bright turquoise [bright turquoise, forest] in last st. *(21 sc)*

Rnds 19 & 21: Rep rnd 3. *(21 sc)*

Fasten off.

BEAK

Row 1: Beg at bottom of Beak with cantaloupe, ch 2, inc in 2nd ch from hook, turn. *(2 sc)*

Row 2: Ch 1, sc in both sc. Fasten off. *(2 sc)*

FOOT

Make 2.

With cantaloupe, ch 15, sc in 2nd ch from hook and each rem ch across. Fasten off. *(14 sc)*

ASSEMBLY & FINISHING

Refer to photo as a guide for placement of pieces.

Position and pin Wings, with Trim facing front, just below color change at base of Head and sew in place across top of Wing with beg or end tail.

Position and pin Beak between eyes. With end tail, sew in place. Bend Feet to create a V-shape with one side slightly longer than the other, with center edges touching only at base of V, position and pin Feet on base of Body, sew in place.

With black thread and using **straight stitches** *(see illustration)*, embroider an eyebrow slightly angled over each eye. Weave in rem ends. ●

Straight Stitch

Fun Fact

Budgies can swivel their heads 180 degrees due to having extra vertebrae in their necks.

Harriet the Hamster

Harriet is quite the athlete! Most days, you can find her running, climbing and setting records on the obstacle course.

SKILL LEVEL
Easy

FINISHED MEASUREMENTS
4 inches wide across Body x 6 inches tall

MATERIALS
- Scheepjes Softfun light (DK) weight cotton/acrylic yarn (1¾ oz/153 yds/50g per ball): 1 ball each #2621 mustard, #2530 cloud and #2513 light rose or #2491 pecan, #2530 cloud and #2513 light rose*
- Size D/3/3.25mm crochet hook or size needed to obtain gauge
- Tapestry needle
- Stitch marker
- 9mm safety eye: 2**
- Black thread
- Polyester fiberfill

Purchase indicated colors for the Hamster(s) of your choice.
**For use by children under 3 years of age, embroider eyes with black thread.*

GAUGE
10 sc = 1½ inches; 10 rows = 2 inches

PATTERN NOTES
Instructions given are for first hamster; changes for 2nd hamster are in brackets. Where only 1 color is given, it applies to both hamsters.

Pieces are worked separately, then sewn together unless otherwise stated.

All pieces begin with slip ring, chain 1 and indicated number of single crochet worked in ring. Pull gently on beginning tail to close ring after round 1 is completed. If desired, begin instead with 2 chains and indicated number of single crochet worked in 2nd chain from hook.

Work in continuous rounds; do not join unless instructed to do so. Place marker in first stitch of round and move up as work progresses.

Weave in ends as work progresses.

To change color in indicated single crochet, work last yarn over with **new color** (see illustration). Drop color not in use to back of work until next needed or cut, whichever is indicated.

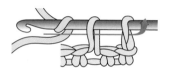

Single Crochet Color Change

Stuff firmly, but not so stuffing shows through stitches.

Leave long tails for sewing when fastening off pieces that require assembly.

SPECIAL STITCHES
Increase (inc): 2 sc in indicated st.

Invisible single crochet decrease (inv dec): Insert hook in **front lp** (see Stitch Guide) of next 2 sts, yo, pull up a lp, yo, draw through 2 lps on hook.

HAMSTER
HEAD & BODY
Rnd 1: Beg at top of Head with mustard [pecan], form a **slip ring** (see illustration on page 24), ch 1, 6 sc in ring or **ch 2, 6 sc in 2nd ch from hook** (see Pattern Notes). **Do not join, place marker in first sc** (see Pattern Notes). (6 sc)

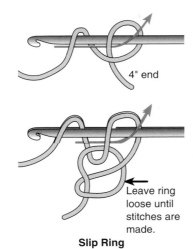

Slip Ring

4" end

Leave ring loose until stitches are made.

Rnd 2: Inc *(see Special Stitches)* in each st around. *(12 sc)*

Rnd 3: [Sc in next sc, inc in next sc] 6 times. *(18 sc)*

Rnd 4: [Sc in next sc, inc in next sc] 9 times. *(27 sc)*

Rnd 5: Sc in each sc around. *(27 sc)*

Rnd 6: [Sc in next 2 sc, inc in next sc] 9 times. *(36 sc)*

Rnds 7 & 8: Rep rnd 5. *(36 sc)*

Rnd 9: [Sc in next 3 sc, inc in next sc] 9 times. *(45 sc)*

Rnds 10–13: Rep rnd 4. *(45 sc)*

Rnd 14: [Sc in next 7 sc, **inv dec** *(see Special Stitches)* in next sc] 5 times. *(40 sc)*

Fun Fact

Hamsters hoard their food in their cheeks. They can expand their cheek pouches to nearly triple their size. They can also fill their cheeks with air to help them float in water.

Rnd 15: Sc in next 13 sc, place first safety eye in last sc made, sc in next 6 sc, place 2nd safety eye in last st made, sc in next 21 sc. *(40 sc)*

Rnd 16: Sc color change *(see illustration and Pattern Notes)* to cloud in next sc, rep rnd 5. Cut mustard [pecan]. *(40 sc)*

Rnds 17 & 18: Rep rnd 5. *(40 sc)*

Rnd 19: [Sc in next 6 sc, inv dec in next 2 sts] 5 times. *(35 sc)*

Rnds 20 & 21: Rep rnd 5. *(35 sc)*

Rnd 22: Sc in next sc, [inv dec in next 2 sts] 17 times. *(18 sc)*

Stuff *(see Pattern Notes)* Head.

Rnd 23: Sc color change to mustard [pecan] in next sc, sc in same sc, inc in next 17 sc. Cut cloud. *(36 sc)*

Rnd 24: [Sc in next 5 sc, inc in next sc] 6 times. *(42 sc)*

Rnds 25–30: Rep rnd 5. *(42 sc)*

Rnd 31: [Sc in next 6 sc, inc in next sc] 6 times. *(48 sc)*

Rnd 32: Inv dec in next 2 sc around. *(24 sc)*

Rnds 33 & 34: Rep rnd 5. *(24 sc)*

Rnd 35: [Inv dec in next 2 sc] around. *(12 sc)*

Stuff Body.

Rnds 36 & 37: Inv dec in next 2 sc around. At end of last rnd, fasten off. *(3 sc)*

EAR
Make 2.

Rnd 1: With light rose, form a slip ring, ch 1, 6 sc in ring or ch 2, 6 sc in 2nd ch from hook. Do not join, place marker in first sc. *(6 sc)*

Rnd 2: Sc color change to mustard [pecan] in next sc, sc in same sc, inc in each sc around. Cut light rose. **Fasten off** *(see Pattern Notes)* mustard [pecan]. *(12 sc)*

ARM
Make 2.

Rnd 1: Beg at tip of Arm with light rose, form a slip ring, ch 1, 6 sc in ring or ch 2, 6 sc in 2nd ch from hook. Do not join, place marker in first sc. *(6 sc)*

Rnd 2: Sc color change to mustard [pecan] in next sc, sc in same sc, inc in each sc around. Cut light rose. *(6 sc)*

Rnd 3: Inc in next sc, sc in next 5 sc. *(7 sc)*

Rnds 4 & 5: Sc in each sc around. *(7 sc)*

Rnd 6: Inc in next sc, sc in next 6 sc. Fasten off. *(8 sc)*

LEG
Make 2.

Rnd 1: Beg at tip of Leg with light rose, form a slip ring, ch 1, 6 sc in ring or ch 2, 6 sc in 2nd ch from hook. Do not join, place marker in first sc. *(6 sc)*

Rnd 2: Sc color change to mustard [pecan], [inc in next sc, sc in next 2 sc] twice. Cut light rose. *(8 sc)*

Rnds 3–5: Sc in each sc around. Fasten off. *(8 sc)*

ASSEMBLY & FINISHING
Refer to photo as a guide for placement of pieces.

Stuff all pieces.

Sew Arms and Legs in place.

Position Ears on sides of Head and sew in place.

With black thread, embroider **straight stitches** *(see illustration)* for mouth and eyebrows. ●

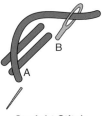

Straight Stitch

Teddy the Turtle

Teddy and his pals can be found swimming in the open water and sunning on the beach, chatting and sipping their favorite beverages.

Fun Fact

Turtles do not have teeth. They use their beaks to grasp their food. Their beaks are made of keratin just like our fingernails.

SKILL LEVEL
Easy

FINISHED MEASUREMENTS
4 inches wide across Shells x 4 inches tall

MATERIALS

- Scheepjes Softfun light (DK) weight cotton/acrylic yarn (1¾ oz/153 yds/50g per ball):
  1 ball each #2535 forest and #2639 green tea, #2616 pickle and #2531 olive or #2639 green tea and #2412 snow*
  Small amount each #2634 bumblebee and #2621 mustard (for Barnacles)
- Size D/3/3.25mm crochet hook or size needed to obtain gauge
- Tapestry needle
- Stitch marker
- 9mm safety eye: 2**
- Black thread
- Polyester fiberfill

*Purchase indicated color pair(s) for the Turtle(s) of your choice.
**For use by children under 3 years of age, embroider eyes with black thread.

GAUGE
10 sc = 1½ inches; 10 rows = 2 inches

PATTERN NOTES
Instructions given are for first pair of colors; changes for 2nd and 3rd pairs are in brackets.

Pieces are worked separately, then sewn together unless otherwise stated.

All pieces begin with slip ring, chain 1 and indicated number of single crochet worked in ring. Pull gently on beginning tail to close ring after round 1 is completed. If desired, begin instead with 2 chains and indicated number of single crochet worked in 2nd chain from hook. Work in continuous rounds; do not join unless instructed to do so. Place marker in first stitch of round and move up as work progresses.

Weave in ends as work progresses.

Leave long tails for sewing when fastening off pieces which require assembly.

Stuff firmly, but not so stuffing shows through stitches.

SPECIAL STITCHES
Increase (inc): 2 sc in indicated st.

Invisible single crochet decrease (inv dec): Insert hook in **front lp** (see Stitch Guide) of each of next 2 sts, yo, pull up a lp, yo, draw through 2 lps on hook.

Single crochet join (sc join): Place a slip knot on hook, insert hook in indicated st, yo, pull up a lp, yo and draw through both lps on hook.

TURTLE
TOP SHELL
Rnd 1: Beg at top of Shell with forest [pickle, olive], form a **slip ring** (see illustration), ch 1, 6 sc in ring or **ch 2, 6 sc in 2nd ch from hook** (see

Pattern Notes). **Do not join, place marker in first sc** (see Pattern Notes). (6 sc)

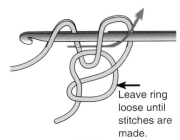

Leave ring loose until stitches are made.

Slip Ring

Rnd 2: Inc (see Special Stitches) in each st around. (12 sc)

Rnd 3: [Sc in next sc, inc in next sc] 6 times. (18 sc)

Rnd 4: Sc in each sc around. (18 sc)

Rnd 5: [Sc in next sc, inc in next sc] 9 times. (27 sc)

Rnd 6: [Sc in next 2 sc, inc in next sc] 9 times. (36 sc)

Rnd 7: Rep rnd 4. (36 sc)

Rnd 8: [Sc in next sc, inc in next sc] 18 times. (54 sc)

Rnds 9–11: Rep rnd 4. (54 sc)

Rnd 12: Sc in next 4 sc, [sc in next 3 sc, **inv dec** (see Special Stitches) in next 2 sc] 10 times. (44 sc)

Rnds 13–15: Rep rnd 4. At end of last rnd. Leaving 6-inch tail, fasten off at end of last rnd. (44 sc)

BOTTOM SHELL
Rnd 1: Beg at bottom of Shell with forest [pickle, olive], form a slip ring,

ch 1, 6 sc in ring or ch 2, 6 sc in 2nd ch from hook. Do not join, place marker in first sc. *(6 sc)*

Rnd 2: Inc in each st around. *(12 sc)*

Rnd 3: [Sc in next sc, inc in next sc] 6 times. *(18 sc)*

Rnd 4: [Sc in next 2 sc, inc in next sc] 6 times. *(24 sc)*

Rnd 5: [Sc in next sc, inc in next sc] 12 times. *(36 sc)*

Rnd 6: [Sc in next 6 sc, inc in next sc] 5 times, sc in next sc. *(41 sc)*

Rnd 7: Sc in next sc, [sc in next 12 sc, inc in next sc] 3 times, sc in next sc. Leaving 6-inch tail, fasten off. *(44 sc)*

HEAD

Rnd 1: Beg at top of Head with green tea [olive, snow], form a slip ring, ch 1, 6 sc in ring or ch 2, 6 sc in 2nd ch from hook. Do not join, place marker in first sc. *(6 sc)*

Rnd 2: Inc in each st around. *(12 sc)*

Rnd 3: [Sc in next sc, inc in next sc] 6 times. *(18 sc)*

Rnd 4: [Sc in next 2 sc, inc in next sc] 6 times. *(24 sc)*

Rnd 5: [Sc in next 3 sc, inc in next sc] 6 times. *(30 sc)*

Rnds 6 & 7: Sc in each sc around. *(30 sc)*

Rnd 8: [Sc in next 4 sc, inv dec in next 2 sc] 5 times. *(25 sc)*

Rnd 9: Rep rnd 6. *(25 sc)*

Rnd 10: Sc in next 11 sc, place first safety eye in last sc made, sc in next 4 sc, place 2nd safety eye in last st made, sc in next 10 sc. *(25 sc)*

Rnds 11–14: Rep rnd 6. *(25 sc)*

Rnd 15: Sc in next sc, [inv dec in next 2 sc] 12 times. *(13 sc)*

Stuff *(see Pattern Notes)* Head.

Rnd 16: [Inv dec in next 2 sc] 6 times, sc in next sc. *(7 sc)*

Rnd 17: Sc in next sc, [inv dec in next 2 sc] 3 times. **Fasten off** *(see Pattern Notes)*. *(4 sc)*

FLIPPER
Make 4.

Rnd 1: With green tea [olive, snow], form a slip ring, ch 1, 6 sc in ring or ch 2, 6 sc in 2nd ch from hook. Do not join, place marker in first sc. *(6 sc)*

Rnd 2: Inc in each st around. *(12 sc)*

Rnd 3: [Sc in next sc, inc in next sc] 6 times. *(18 sc)*

Rnd 4: [Sc in next sc, inc in next sc] 9 times. *(27 sc)*

Row 5: With WS tog, fold Flipper in half, working through both thicknesses of curved edge, sc in next 13 sc. Fasten off. *(13 sc)*

BARNACLE
Small Patch
Make 1 each with forest, bumblebee and mustard.

Form a slip ring, ch 1, 6 sc in ring or ch 2, 6 sc in 2nd ch from hook. Fasten off. *(6 sc)*

Large Patch
Make 2 with choice of snow, bumblebee, mustard, forest and green tea.

Rnd 1: Form a slip ring, ch 1, 6 sc in ring or ch 2, 6 sc in 2nd ch from hook. *(6 sc)*

Rnd 2: [Sc in next sc, inc in next sc] 3 times. Fasten off. *(9 sc)*

ASSEMBLY & FINISHING
Refer to photo as a guide for placement of pieces.

Holding Shells with WS tog and working through both thicknesses of last rnds, **sc join** *(see Special Stitches)* matching color in any st, stuffing as work progresses, sc in each st around. Fasten off.

Adding more stuffing to Head as needed, sew Head to Top Shell.

Sew Barnacles with edges touching on side of Top Shell.

Sew Flippers to joined edge of Shells.

With black thread, embroider 1 **straight stitches** *(see illustration)* for mouth and 2 stitches for eyebrows. ●

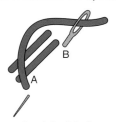

Straight Stitch

Trudy the Tarantula

Trudy is no social butterfly; you can often find her relaxing in a shady crack or burrow.

SKILL LEVEL
Easy

FINISHED MEASUREMENTS
3½ inches wide across Body, excluding legs x 5 inches long

MATERIALS
- Scheepjes Softfun light (DK) weight cotton/acrylic yarn (1¾ oz/153 yds/50g per ball): 1 ball each in #2601 graphite and #2621 mustard
- Size D/3/3.25mm crochet hook or size needed to obtain gauge
- Tapestry needle
- Stitch marker
- 9mm safety eye: 2*
- 12mm safety eye: 2*
- Long pins
- 11-inch-long 9-gauge wire: 4 pieces
- Black thread
- Polyester fiberfill

*For use by children under 3 years of age, embroider eyes with black thread.

GAUGE
10 sc = 1½ inches; 10 rows = 2 inches

PATTERN NOTES
Pieces are worked separately then sewn together unless otherwise stated.

All pieces begin with slip ring, chain 1 and indicated number of single crochet worked in ring. Pull gently on beginning tail to close ring after round 1 is completed. If desired, begin instead with 2 chains and indicated number of single crochet worked in 2nd chain from hook.

All pieces are worked in continuous rounds; do not join unless instructed to do so. Place marker in first stitch of round and move up as work progresses.

Stuff firmly, but not so the stuffing shows through the stitches.

To change color in indicated single crochet, work last yarn over with **new color** (see illustration). Drop color not in use to back of work until next needed. Fasten off only when instructed.

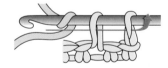

Single Crochet Color Change

Leave long tails when fastening off on pieces that will require assembly. Use these tails for sewing.

SPECIAL STITCHES

Increase (inc): 2 sc in indicated st.

Invisible single crochet decrease (inv dec): Insert hook in front lp of next 2 sts, yo, pull up a lp, yo, draw through 2 lps on hook.

TARANTULA

HEAD

Rnd 1: Beg at top of head with graphite, form a **slip ring** (see illustration), 6 sc in ring or **ch 2, 6 sc in 2nd ch from hook** (see Pattern Notes). (6 sc)

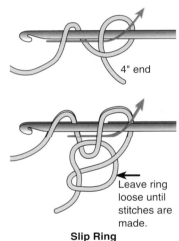

4" end

Leave ring loose until stitches are made.

Slip Ring

Rnd 2: Inc (see Special Stitches) in each sc around. (12 sc)

Rnd 3: [Sc in next sc, inc in next sc] 6 times. (18 sc)

Fun Fact

Some adult tarantulas can survive up to two years without food.

Rnd 4: [Sc in next 2 sc, inc in next sc] 6 times. (24 sc)

Rnd 5: Sc in each sc around. (24 sc)

Rnd 6: [Sc in next 3 sc, inc in next sc] 6 times. (30 sc)

Rnd 7: Sc in next 10 sc, place first 9mm safety eye in last sc made, sc in next 3 sc, place 2nd 9mm safety eye in last sc made, sc in next 17 sc. (30 sc)

Rnd 8: Rep rnd 5. (30 sc)

Rnd 9: Sc in next 9 sc, place first 12mm safety eye in last sc made, sc in next 5 sc, place 2nd 12mm safety in last sc made, sc in next 16 sc. (30 sc)

Rnds 10–14: Rep rnd 5. (30 sc)

Rnd 15: [**Inv dec** (see Special Stitches) in next 2 sc] around. (15 sc)

Stuff (see Pattern Notes) piece firmly.

Rnd 16: [Inv dec in next 2 sc] 7 times, sc in next sc. (8 sc)

Rnd 17: [Inv dec in next 2 sc] 4 times. (4 sc)

Rnd 18: [Inv dec in next 2 sc] twice. Fasten off, weave in ends. (2 sc)

BODY

Rnd 1: Beg at back of Body with graphite, form a slip ring, 6 sc in ring or ch 2, 6 sc in 2nd ch from hook. (6 sc)

Rnd 2: Inc in each sc around. (12 sc)

Rnd 3: [Sc in next sc, inc in next sc] 6 times. (18 sc)

Rnd 4: [Sc in next 2 sc, inc in next sc] 6 times. (24 sc)

Rnd 5: [Sc in next sc, inc in next sc] 12 times. (36 sc)

Rnd 6: [Sc in next 5 sc, inc in next sc] 6 times. (42 sc)

Rnd 7: Sc in next 2 sc, [sc in next 3 sc, inc in next sc] 10 times, **sc color change** (see Pattern Notes) to mustard in last st. (52 sc)

Rnd 8: Sc in each sc around, sc color change to graphite in last st. (52 sc)

Rnd 9: Sc in each sc around, sc color change to mustard in last st. (52 sc)

Rnds 10 & 11: Rep rnds 8 and 9. (52 sc)

Rnd 12: Sc in next 2 sc, [sc in next 3 sc, inv dec in next 2 sc] 10 times. Fasten off mustard. (42 sc)

Rnds 13–15: Sc in each sc around. (42 sc)

Rnd 16: [Inv dec in next 2 sc] around. (21 sc)

Rnd 17: Rep rnd 13. (21 sc)

Rnd 18: Sc in next sc, [inv dec in next 2 sc] 10 times. (11 sc)

Stuff piece firmly.

Rnd 19: [Inv dec in next 2 sc] 5 times, sc in next sc. (6 sc)

Rnd 20: [Inv dec in next 2 sc] around. **Fasten off** (see Pattern Notes). (3 sc)

LEG
Make 8.

Rnd 1: Beg at tip of Leg with graphite, form a slip ring, 6 sc in ring or ch 2, 6 sc in 2nd ch from hook. (6 sc)

Rnd 2: [Sc in next sc, inc in next sc] 3 times. (9 sc)

Rnd 3: Sc in each sc around. (9 sc)

Rnd 4: Inv dec in next 2 sc, sc in next 7 sc. (8 sc)

Rnds 5–25: Rep rnd 3. (8 sc)

Fasten off.

ASSEMBLY & FINISHING

Refer to photo as a guide for placement of pieces.

Tilt Body sideways and use long pins to hold Body in place at back of Head with stripe jog on underside. With

end tail of Body, sew both pieces tog. Slide 3 pieces of wire through Body to position for back 6 Legs, slide 4th wire through Head for front pair of Legs. Bend both ends of each wire so there are no sharp edges. Stuff Legs and place over wire, sew in place.

With black thread, embroider small **backstitches** (see illustration) onto Head, 1 row under bottom eyes, to create a mouth, then embroider a single stitch angled over each top eye to create eyebrows.

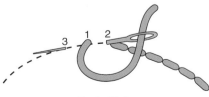

Backstitch

Weave in rem ends. ●

Stella the

Stella the Sugar Glider just learned to fly, admiring the stars while she glides from branch to branch.

SKILL LEVEL
Easy

FINISHED MEASUREMENTS
3½ inches wide across bottom, excluding Arms (6 inches wide with Arms) x 6 inches tall

MATERIALS
- Scheepjes Softfun light (DK) weight cotton/acrylic yarn (1¾ oz/153 yds/50g per ball): 1 ball each #2530 cloud, #2510 dove and #2513 light rose; #2533 wheat, #2510 dove and #2513 light rose; or #2412 snow and #2513 light rose*
- Size D/3/3.25mm crochet hook or size needed to obtain gauge
- Tapestry needle
- Stitch marker
- 9mm safety eye: 2 (black for 3-color doll; pink for albino doll)**
- 11-inch-long 9 gauge wire: 4 pieces
- Black thread
- Polyester fiberfill

Purchase indicated color group(s) for the Sugar Glider(s) of your choice.
**For use by children under 3 years of age, embroider eyes with black or pink thread.*

GAUGE
10 sc = 1½ inches; 10 rows = 2 inches

PATTERN NOTES
Regardless of color, instructions for all pieces are same except for Head. Instructions for albino Head is different from cloud and wheat.

Except for Head, instructions given for all pieces are for first group of colors; changes for 2nd and 3rd groups are in brackets. When color is same in all color combinations or in both 2nd and 3rd groups, that color will be shown once.

Pieces are worked separately, then sewn together unless otherwise stated.

For pieces beginning with slip ring, chain 1 and indicated number of single crochet worked in ring. Pull gently on beginning tail to close ring after round 1 is completed. If desired, begin instead with 2 chains and indicated number of single crochet worked in 2nd chain from hook.

For pieces worked in continuous rounds, do not join unless instructed to do so. Place marker in first stitch of round and move up as work progresses.

Weave in ends as work progresses.

To change color in indicated sc, work last yarn over with **new color**

(see illustration). Drop color not in use to back of work until next needed or cut, whichever is indicated.

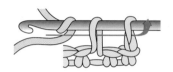

Single Crochet Color Change

Leave long tails for sewing when fastening off pieces which require assembly.

Stuff firmly, but not so stuffing shows through stitches.

SPECIAL STITCHES
Increase (inc): 2 sc in indicated st.

Invisible single crochet decrease (inv dec): Insert hook in **front lp** (see Stitch Guide) of each of next 2 sts, yo, pull up a lp, yo, draw through 2 lps on hook.

SUGAR GLIDER

HEAD
Cloud or Wheat Only
Rnd 1: Beg at tip of nose with light rose, form a **slip ring** (see illustration on page 34), ch 1, 6 sc in ring or **ch 2, 6 sc in 2nd ch from hook** (see Pattern Notes). **Do not join, place marker in first sc** (see Pattern Notes). (6 sc)

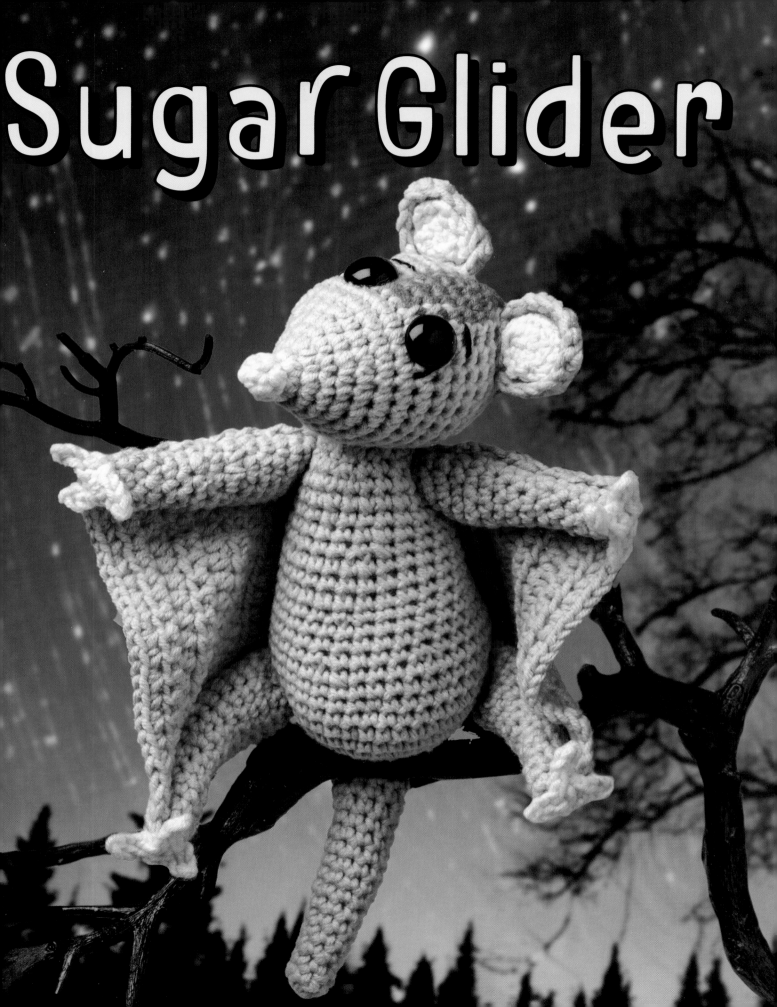

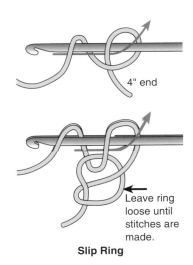

4" end

Leave ring loose until stitches are made.

Slip Ring

Rnds 2 & 3: Sc in each st around. *(6 sc)*

Rnd 4: Sc color change *(see Pattern Notes)* to cloud [wheat] in next sc, **inc** *(see Special Stitches)* in next sc, [sc in next sc, inc in next sc] twice. Cut light rose. *(9 sc)*

Rnd 5: [Sc in next sc, inc in next sc] 4 times, sc in next sc. *(13 sc)*

Rnd 6: Rep rnd 2. *(13 sc)*

Rnd 7: Sc in next sc, [sc in next sc, inc in next sc] 6 times. *(19 sc)*

Rnd 8: Sc in next sc, [sc in next 2 sc, inc in next sc] 6 times. *(25 sc)*

Rnd 9: [Sc in next 4 sc, inc in next sc] 5 times. *(30 sc)*

Rnd 10: Rep rnd 2. *(30 sc)*

Rnd 11: Sc in next 16 sc, place first safety eye in last st made, sc in next 6 sc, place 2nd safety eye in last st made, sc in next 8 sc. *(30 sc)*

Rnd 12: Sc in next 16 sc, change to dove, sc in next 3 sc, change to cloud [wheat], sc in next 11 sc. *(30 sc)*

Rnd 13: Sc in next 15 sc, change to dove, sc in next 5 sc, change to cloud [wheat], sc in next 10 sc. *(30 sc)*

Rnds 14 & 15: Rep rnd 13. *(30 sc)*

Rnd 16: Sc in next 15 sc, change to dove, sc in next 2 sc, inv dec in next

2 sc, sc in next sc, change to cloud [wheat], sc in next 10 sc. *(29 sc)*

Rnd 17: Sc in next 16 sc, change to dove, sc in next 3 sc, change to cloud [wheat], sc in next 10 sc. *(29 sc)*

Rnd 18: Sc in next 16 sc, change to dove, sc in next sc, inv dec in next 2 sc, change to cloud [wheat], sc in next 10 sc. *(28 sc)*

Rnd 19: [Inv dec in next 2 sc] around. *(14 sc)*

Rnd 20: Rep rnd 2. *(14 sc)*

Rnd 21: Inv dec in next 2 sc around. *(7 sc)*

Rnd 22: Sc in next sc, [inv dec in next 2 sc] 3 times. **Fasten off** *(see Pattern Notes).* *(4 sc)*

Albino Only

Rnd 1: Beg at tip of nose with light rose, form a **slip ring** *(see illustration)*, ch 1, 6 sc in ring or **ch 2, 6 sc in 2nd ch from hook** *(see Pattern Notes).* **Do not join, place marker in first sc** *(see Pattern Notes).* *(6 sc)*

Rnds 2 & 3: Sc in each st around. *(6 sc)*

Rnd 4: Sc color change *(see Pattern Notes)* to snow in next sc, **inc** *(see Special Stitches)* in next sc, [sc in next sc, inc in next sc] twice. Cut light rose. *(9 sc)*

Rnd 5: [Sc in next sc, inc in next sc] 4 times, sc in next sc. *(13 sc)*

Rnd 6: Rep rnd 2. *(13 sc)*

Rnd 7: Sc in next sc, [sc in next sc, inc in next sc] 6 times. *(19 sc)*

Rnd 8: Sc in next sc, [sc in next 2 sc, inc in next sc] 6 times. *(25 sc)*

Rnd 9: [Sc in next 4 sc, inc in next sc] 5 times. *(30 sc)*

Rnd 10: Rep rnd 2. *(30 sc)*

Rnd 11: Sc in next 16 sc, place first safety eye in last st made, sc in next 6 sc, place 2nd safety eye in last st made, sc in next 8 sc. *(30 sc)*

Rnds 12–15: Rep rnd 2. *(30 sc)*

Rnd 16: Sc in next 17 sc, **inv dec** *(see Special Stitches)* in next 2 sc, sc in next 11 sc. *(29 sc)*

Rnd 17: Rep rnd 2. *(29 sc)*

Rnd 18: Sc in next 17 sc, inv dec in next 2 sc, sc in next 10 sc. *(28 sc)*

Rnd 19: Inv dec in next 2 sc around. *(14 sc)*

Rnd 20: Rep rnd 2. *(14 sc)*

Rnd 21: Inv dec in next 2 sc around. *(7 sc)*

Rnd 22: Sc in next sc, [inv dec in next 2 sc] 3 times. **Fasten off** *(see Pattern Notes).* *(4 sc)*

EAR
Make 2.

Row 1: Beg at tip of Ear with cloud [wheat, snow], ch 2, 2 sc in 2nd ch from hook, turn. *(2 sc)*

Row 2: Ch 1, inc in both sc, turn. *(4 sc)*

Row 3: Ch 1, sc in each sc across, turn. *(4 sc)*

Row 4: Ch 1, inc in first sc, sc in next 2 sc, inc in last sc, turn. *(6 sc)*

Row 5: Rep row 3. *(6 sc)*

Row 6: Ch 1, inv dec in first 2 sc, sc in next 2 sc, inv dec in last 2 sc, do not turn. *(4 sc)*

Rnd 7: Working in sts and ends of rows, sc 17 evenly around Ear. Fasten off. *(17 sc)*

INNER EAR
Make 2.

Row 1: Beg at tip of Inner Ear with light rose, ch 2, 2 sc in 2nd ch from hook, turn. *(2 sc)*

Row 2: Ch 1, inc in both sc, turn. *(4 sc)*

Row 3: Ch 1, sc in each sc across, turn. *(4 sc)*

Row 4: Ch 1, inv dec in first 2 sc, inv dec in last 2 sc. Fasten off. *(2 sc)*

BODY

Rnd 1: Beg at bottom of Body with cloud [wheat, snow], form a slip ring, 6 sc in ring or ch 2, 6 sc in 2nd ch from hook. *(6 sc)*

Rnd 2: Inc in each sc around. *(12 sc)*

Rnd 3: [Sc in next sc, inc in next sc] 6 times. *(18 sc)*

Rnd 4: [Sc in next 2 sc, inc in next sc] 6 times. *(24 sc)*

Rnd 5: Sc in each sc around. *(24 sc)*

Rnd 6: [Sc in next sc, inc in next sc] twice. *(36 sc)*

Rnds 7–12: Rep rnd 5. *(36 sc)*

Rnd 13: [Sc in next 4 sc, inv dec in next 2 sc] 6 times. *(30 sc)*

Rnds 14 & 15: Rep rnd 5. *(30 sc)*

Rnd 16: [Sc in next 8 sc, inv dec in next 2 sc] 3 times. *(27 sc)*

Rnds 17–19: Rep rnd 5. *(27 sc)*

Rnd 20: Sc in next 2 sc, [inv dec in next 2 sc, sc in next 3 sc] 5 times. *(22 sc)*

Rnds 21–24: Rep rnd 5. *(22 sc)*

Rnd 25: Sc in next 2 sc, [sc in next 2 sc, inv dec in next 2 sc] 5 times. Fasten off. *(17 sc)*

ARM
Make 4.

Rnd 1: Beg at bottom of Arm with cloud [dove, snow], form a slip ring, 6 sc in ring or ch 2, 6 sc in 2nd ch from hook. *(6 sc)*

Rnd 2: Inc in next sc, sc in next 5 sc. *(7 sc)*

Rnds 3–7: Sc in each sc around. *(7 sc)*

Rnd 8: Sc in next sc, [inc in next sc, sc in next 2 sc] twice. *(9 sc)*

Rnds 9 & 10: Rep rnd 3. *(9 sc)*

Rnd 11: [Inc in next sc, sc in next 2 sc] 3 times. *(12 sc)*

Rnds 12–15: Sc in each sc around. Fasten off at end of last rnd. *(12 sc)*

WING

Make 2.

Row 1: With cloud [dove, snow], ch 21, hdc in 2nd ch from hook and in each ch across, turn. *(20 hdc)*

Rows 2–8: Ch 1, hdc in first hdc and in each hdc across, turn. *(20 hdc)*

Row 9: Ch 1, sc in first hdc, inc in next hdc, [sc in next hdc, inc in next hdc] 9 times, fasten off. *(30 sc)*

TAIL

Rnd 1: Beg at tip of Tail with cloud [dove, snow], form a slip ring, 6 sc in ring, ch 2, 6 sc in 2nd ch from hook. *(6 sc)*

Rnds 2 & 3: Sc in each sc around. *(6 sc)*

Rnd 4: [Inc in next sc, sc in next 2 sc] twice. *(8 sc)*

Rnds 5–7: Rep rnd 2. *(8 sc)*

Rnd 8: [Sc in next 3 sc, inc in next sc] twice. *(10 sc)*

Rnds 9–14: Rep rnd 2. *(10 sc)*

Rnd 15: [Sc in next 4 sc, inc in next sc] twice. *(12 sc)*

Rnds 16–22: Rep rnd 2. *(12 sc)*

Rnd 23: [Sc in next 5 sc, inc in next sc] twice. *(14 sc)*

Rnds 24–26: Rep rnd 2. *(14 sc)*

Rnd 27: [Sc in next 6 sc, inc in next sc] twice. *(16 sc)*

Rnd 28: [Sc in next 7 sc, inc in next sc] twice. *(18 sc)*

Rnd 29: Rep rnd 2. Fasten off. *(18 sc)*

PAW

Make 4.

With light rose, ch 3, slip st in 2nd ch from hook, [ch 3, sl st in 2nd ch from hook and next ch] 3 times, join with sl st in first ch of beg ch-3. Fasten off.

ASSEMBLY & FINISHING

Refer to photo as a guide for placement of pieces.

Stuff Head, Body, Arms and Legs.

Sew Head to Body.

Insert wire in Body where Arms and Legs will be placed. Bend ends of each wire so there are no sharp points. Place Arms and Legs over wires and sew in place.

With WS of Inner Ears and RS of Ears held tog, sew pieces tog, then sew Ears on Head.

Sew Tail to Body.

Extend Arms and Legs horizontally and evenly sp apart. With last rnd of Wings as outer edge, pin Wings across underside of Arms, down Body and across topside of Legs, sew in place.

Sew Paws to tips of Arms and Legs.

With black thread, embroider small **straight stitches** *(see illustration)* for eyebrows on cloud [wheat] Head and, on cloud Head only, eyelashes on outer edge of eyes. ●

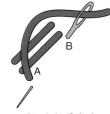

Straight Stitch

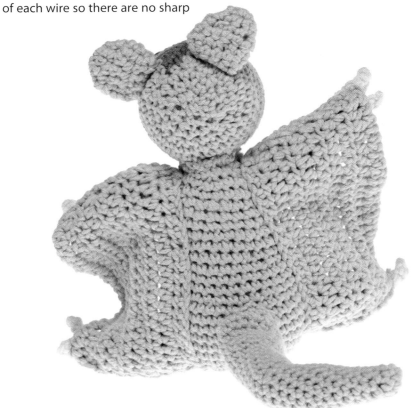

Notes

Metric Conversion Charts

METRIC CONVERSIONS

yards	x	.9144	=	meters (m)
yards	x	91.44	=	centimeters (cm)
inches	x	2.54	=	centimeters (cm)
inches	x	25.40	=	millimeters (mm)
inches	x	.0254	=	meters (m)

centimeters	x	.3937	=	inches
meters	x	1.0936	=	yards

INCHES INTO MILLIMETERS & CENTIMETERS (Rounded off slightly)

inches	mm	cm	inches	cm	inches	cm	inches	cm
1/8	3	0.3	5	12.5	21	53.5	38	96.5
1/4	6	0.6	5 1/2	14	22	56	39	99
3/8	10	1	6	15	23	58.5	40	101.5
1/2	13	1.3	7	18	24	61	41	104
5/8	15	1.5	8	20.5	25	63.5	42	106.5
3/4	20	2	9	23	26	66	43	109
7/8	22	2.2	10	25.5	27	68.5	44	112
1	25	2.5	11	28	28	71	45	114.5
1 1/4	32	3.2	12	30.5	29	73.5	46	117
1 1/2	38	3.8	13	33	30	76	47	119.5
1 3/4	45	4.5	14	35.5	31	79	48	122
2	50	5	15	38	32	81.5	49	124.5
2 1/2	65	6.5	16	40.5	33	84	50	127
3	75	7.5	17	43	34	86.5		
3 1/2	90	9	18	46	35	89		
4	100	10	19	48.5	36	91.5		
4 1/2	115	11.5	20	51	37	94		

KNITTING NEEDLES CONVERSION CHART

Canada/U.S.	0	1	2	3	4	5	6	7	8	9	10	10½	11	13	15
Metric (mm)	2	2¼	2¾	3¼	3½	3¾	4	4½	5	5½	6	6½	8	9	10

CROCHET HOOKS CONVERSION CHART

Canada/U.S.	1/B	2/C	3/D	4/E	5/F	6/G	7	8/H	9/I	10/J	10½/K	N
Metric (mm)	2.25	2.75	3.25	3.5	3.75	4	4.5	5	5.5	6	6.5	9.0

STITCH GUIDE

STITCH ABBREVIATIONS

beg . . . . begin/begins/beginning
bpdc . . . . back post double crochet
bpsc . . . . .back post single crochet
bptr. . . . . .back post treble crochet
CC. . . . . contrasting color
ch(s) . . . . .chain(s)
ch- . . . . .refers to chain or space
    previously made (i.e., ch-1 space)
ch sp(s) . . . . chain space(s)
cl(s) . . . . cluster(s)
cm . . . . centimeter(s)
dc . . . . double crochet (singular/plural)
dc dec. . . . . double crochet 2 or more
    stitches together, as indicated
dec. . . . . decrease/decreases/decreasing
dtr . . . . double treble crochet
ext . . . . .extended
fpdc. . . . . front post double crochet
fpsc . . . . front post single crochet
fptr . . . . front post treble crochet
g . . . . gram(s)
hdc . . . . half double crochet
hdc dec . . . . half double crochet 2 or more
    stitches together, as indicated
inc . . . . increase/increases/increasing
lp(s) . . . . loop(s)
MC . . . . main color
mm . . . . .millimeter(s)
oz . . . . ounce(s)
pc . . . . popcorn(s)
rem. . . . . remain/remains/remaining
rep(s) . . . . .repeat(s)
rnd(s). . . . . .round(s)
RS . . . . right side
sc . . . . single crochet (singular/plural)
sc dec . . . . .single crochet 2 or more
    stitches together, as indicated
sk . . . . skip/skipped/skipping
sl st(s) . . . . slip stitch(es)
sp(s) . . . . space(s)/spaced
st(s) . . . . stitch(es)
tog . . . . together
tr. . . . . treble crochet
trtr . . . . triple treble
WS . . . . wrong side
yd(s) . . . . .yard(s)
yo . . . . yarn over

YARN CONVERSION

OUNCES TO GRAMS	GRAMS TO OUNCES
1 . . . . .28.4	25 . . . . ⅞
2 . . . . .56.7	40 . . . . 1⅔
3 . . . . .85.0	50 . . . . 1¾
4 . . . . 113.4	100 . . . . 3½

UNITED STATES		UNITED KINGDOM
sl st (slip stitch)	=	sc (single crochet)
sc (single crochet)	=	dc (double crochet)
hdc (half double crochet)	=	htr (half treble crochet)
dc (double crochet)	=	tr (treble crochet)
tr (treble crochet)	=	dtr (double treble crochet)
dtr (double treble crochet)	=	ttr (triple treble crochet)
skip	=	miss

Reverse single crochet (reverse sc): Ch 1, sk first st, working from left to right, insert hook in next st from front to back, draw up lp on hook, yo and draw through both lps on hook.

Chain (ch): Yo, pull through lp on hook.

Single crochet (sc): Insert hook in st, yo, pull through st, yo, pull through both lps on hook.

Double crochet (dc): Yo, insert hook in st, yo, pull through st, [yo, pull through 2 lps] twice.

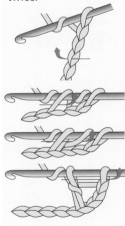

Front loop (front lp): Back loop (back lp):

Front Loop   Back Loop

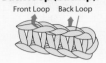

Front post stitch (fp): Back post stitch (bp): When working post st, insert hook from right to left around post of st on previous row.

Back   Front

← Post of Stitch

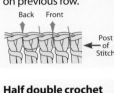

Half double crochet (hdc): Yo, insert hook in st, yo, pull through st, yo, pull through all 3 lps on hook.

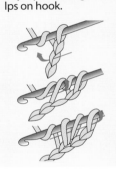

Double treble crochet (dtr): Yo 3 times, insert hook in st, yo, pull through st, [yo, pull through 2 lps] 4 times.

Slip stitch (sl st): Insert hook in st, pull through both lps on hook.

Chain color change (ch color change): Yo with new color, draw through last lp on hook.

Double crochet color change (dc color change): Drop first color, yo with new color, draw through last 2 lps of st.

Treble crochet (tr): Yo twice, insert hook in st, yo, pull through st, [yo, pull through 2 lps] 3 times.

Single crochet decrease (sc dec): (Insert hook, yo, draw lp through) in each of the sts indicated, yo, draw through all lps on hook.

Example of 2-sc dec

Half double crochet decrease (hdc dec): (Yo, insert hook, yo, draw lp through) in each of the sts indicated, yo, draw through all lps on hook.

Example of 2-hdc dec

Double crochet decrease (dc dec): (Yo, insert hook, yo, draw lp through, yo, draw through 2 lps on hook) in each of the sts indicated, yo, draw through all lps on hook.

Example of 2-dc dec

Treble crochet decrease (tr dec): Holding back last lp of each st, tr in each of the sts indicated, yo, pull through all lps on hook.

Example of 2-tr dec

39

Jackie Laing is the designer behind Amidorable Crochet. She's been playing with yarn, making amigurumi creations and sharing patterns since 2009. Her inspiration for her designs comes from her love for animals, movies and music! She enjoys crocheting with her daughter, who introduced her to the craft, and her partner who also takes part in this wonderful art!

Putting love into amigurumi, one stitch at a time ♥.

Annie's® Published by Annie's, 306 East Parr Road, Berne, IN 46711. Printed in USA. Copyright © 2024 Annie's. All rights reserved. This publication may not be reproduced in part or in whole without written permission from the publisher.

RETAIL STORES: If you would like to carry this publication or any other Annie's publication, visit AnniesWSL.com.

Every effort has been made to ensure that the instructions in this publication are complete and accurate. We cannot, however, take responsibility for human error, typographical mistakes or variations in individual work. Please visit AnniesCustomerService.com to check for pattern updates.

ISBN: 979-8-89253-319-5
1 2 3 4 5 6 7 8 9